SIMON PETER
LEADER GUIDE

SIMON PETER:
FLAWED BUT FAITHFUL DISCIPLE

Simon Peter: Flawed but Faithful Disciple
978-1-5018-4598-7 Hardcover with jacket
978-1-5018-4599-4 eBook
978-1-5018-4600-7 Large Print

Simon Peter: DVD
978-1-5018-4603-8

Simon Peter: Leader Guide
978-1-5018-4601-4
978-1-5018-4602-1 eBook

Simon Peter: Youth Edition
978-1-5018-4610-6
978-1-5018-4611-3 eBook

Simon Peter: Children's Leader Guide
978-1-5018-4612-0

Also by Adam Hamilton

24 Hours That Changed the World

Christianity and World Religions

Christianity's Family Tree

Confronting the Controversies

Creed

Enough

Faithful

Final Words from the Cross

Forgiveness

Half Truths

John

Leading Beyond the Walls

Love to Stay

Making Sense of the Bible

Moses

Not a Silent Night

Revival

Seeing Gray in a World
of Black and White

Selling Swimsuits in the Arctic

Speaking Well

The Call

The Journey

The Way

Unafraid

Unleashing the Word

When Christians Get It Wrong

Why?

For more information, visit www.AdamHamilton.org

ADAM HAMILTON

Author of *The Call* and *Moses*

SIMON PETER

FLAWED BUT FAITHFUL DISCIPLE

Leader Guide
by Clara Welch

Abingdon Press / Nashville

Simon Peter:
Flawed but Faithful Disciple
Leader Guide

18 19 20 21 22 23 24 25 26 27—10 9 8 7 6 5 4 3 2 1
MANUFACTURED IN THE UNITED STATES OF AMERICA

CONTENTS

TO THE LEADER

Welcome! Thank you for accepting the invitation to serve as the facilitator for this study of *Simon Peter: Flawed but Faithful Disciple* by Adam Hamilton. You and your group of learners will journey together toward a greater understanding of Simon Peter, the man Jesus called to be the "Rock" on which he built his church.

During this six-session study, Adam Hamilton invites his readers to consider the person of Simon Peter from several perspectives. In session 1 we will consider "The Call of the Fisherman." In session 2 we will learn more about the man who stepped out of a boat onto a stormy sea to walk to Jesus. Session 3 offers the opportunity to see Peter as a "stumbling block" to Jesus as well as the "bedrock" on which Jesus built his church. In session 4, we will consider Peter's painful experience of denying Jesus three times on the night of his arrest. The focus of session 5 is Jesus' forgiveness and reinstatement of Peter after the Resurrection. Session 6, titled "The Rest of the Story," includes Scripture passages about Peter's work as a faithful disciple and witness for Christ after Jesus' ascension and the gift of the Holy Spirit.

This six-session study makes use of the following components:

- the book *Simon Peter: Flawed but Faithful Disciple* by Adam Hamilton,
- this Leader Guide,
- a DVD with video segments for each of the six chapters in the book.

It will be helpful if participants obtain a copy of the book in advance and read chapter 1 before the first session. Each participant will need a Bible. A notebook or journal is also recommended for taking notes, recording insights, and noting questions during the study.

Session Format

Every group is different. These session plans have been designed to give you flexibility and choices. A variety of activities and discussion questions are included. As you plan each session, keep the session goals in mind and select the activities and discussion questions that will be most meaningful for your group.

You will want to read the section titled "Before the Session" several days in advance of your meeting time. A few activities suggest making some preparations in advance.

The activities in "Getting Started" are designed to help participants begin to focus on the main topics for the session. They also serve as group building exercises. Watch your time here so you will have time for the in-depth study later in the session.

In many cases, your session time will be too short to do everything that is suggested here.

Select ahead of time which activities best fit the personality of the group and decide how much time you want to allow for each part of the session plan.

The activities in "Wrapping Up" are designed to give participants the opportunity to reflect on and process the various themes and topics covered in the session, as these relate to their own growing relationship with Jesus Christ.

Each session plan follows this outline:

- Planning the Session
  - ◊ Session Goals
  - ◊ Biblical Foundation
  - ◊ Before the Session
- Getting Started
  - ◊ Opening Activities
  - ◊ Opening Prayer
- Learning Together
  - ◊ Video Study and Discussion
  - ◊ Bible Study and Discussion
  - ◊ Book Study and Discussion
  - ◊ Optional Activity/Activities
- Wrapping Up
  - ◊ Closing Activity
  - ◊ Closing Prayer

Preparing for the Session

As you prepare for each session, be sure to do the following:

- Pray for the leading of the Holy Spirit as you prepare for the study. Pray for discernment for yourself and for each member of the study group.
- Before each session, familiarize yourself with the content. Read the book chapter again and watch the video segment.
- Choose the session elements you will use during the group session, including the specific discussion questions you plan to cover. Be prepared, however, to adjust the session as group members interact and as questions arise. Prepare carefully, but allow space for the Holy Spirit to move in and through the material, the group members, and you as facilitator.
- Secure in advance a TV and DVD player or a computer with projection.

- Prepare the space so that it will enhance the learning process. Ideally, group members should be seated around a table or in a circle so that all can see each other. Movable chairs are best, because the group will often be forming pairs or small groups for discussion.
- Bring a supply of Bibles for those who forget to bring their own. Having a variety of translations is helpful.
- For each session you will also need a whiteboard and markers, a chalkboard and chalk, or an easel with paper and markers.

Shaping the Learning Environment

Here are some helpful tips to keep in mind as you lead each session:

- Begin and end on time. If a session is running longer than expected, get consensus from the group before continuing beyond the agreed-upon ending time.
- Create a climate of openness, encouraging group members to participate as they feel comfortable. Remember that some people will jump right in with answers and comments, while others will need time to process what is being discussed.
- If you notice that some group members don't enter the conversation, ask them if they have thoughts to share. Give everyone a chance to talk, but keep the conversation moving. Try to prevent a few individuals from doing all the talking.
- Communicate the importance of group discussions and group exercises.
- If no one answers at first during discussions, don't be afraid of pauses. Count silently to ten; then say something such as "Would anyone like to go first?" If no one responds, venture an answer yourself and ask for comments.
- Model openness as you share with the group. Group members will follow your example. If you limit your sharing to a surface level, others will follow suit.

- Encourage multiple answers or responses before moving on.
- Ask, "Why?" or "Why do you believe that?" or "Can you say more about that?" to help continue a discussion and give it greater depth.
- Affirm others' responses with comments such as "Great" or "Thanks" or "Good insight"—especially if this is the first time someone has spoken during the group session.
- Monitor your own contributions. If you find yourself doing most of the talking, back off so that you don't train the group to listen rather than speak up.
- Remember that you don't have all the answers. Your job is to keep the discussion going and encourage participation.
- Involve group members in various aspects of the group session, such as playing the DVD, saying prayers, or reading the Scripture.
- Note that the session plans sometimes call for breaking into smaller groups. This gives everyone a chance to speak and participate fully. Mix up the teams; don't let the same people pair up on every activity.
- Because many activities call for personal sharing, confidentiality is essential. Group members should never pass along stories that have been shared in the group. Remind the group members at each session: confidentiality is crucial to the success of this study.

We hope this study will help you see yourself in Simon Peter, the flawed but ultimately faithful disciple.

1

THE CALL OF THE FISHERMAN

Planning the Session

Session Goals

Through conversation, activities, and reflection, participants will:

- gain an understanding of the cultural context in which Simon Peter lived,
- discover the skills God may be calling them to use to fish for people,
- and consider the implication of the phrase "But because you say so" (Luke 5:5) for Simon Peter's life and for their lives.

Biblical Foundation

Luke 5:1-11

Before the Session

- Set up a table in the room with name tags, markers, Bibles, extra copies of *Simon Peter*, paper, and pencils.

- Have a whiteboard or chart paper and markers or a chalkboard and chalk available for use during the session.
- On a board or piece of chart paper make two columns. Write "shallow water" at the top of the first column and "deep water" at the top of the second column. This will be used during the "Bible Study and Discussion."
- You may want to write the three types of fishing on a board or chart paper for the "Leading into the Study" activity.

Getting Started

Opening Activities

Greet participants as they arrive. Invite them to make a name tag and pick up a Bible and/or copy of *Simon Peter* if they did not bring one.

Introductions

Introduce yourself. You may want to share why you are excited about teaching this Bible study about Simon Peter.

If you sense that the participants in your group do not know each other well, allow time for them to introduce themselves and share something about their relationship with the church—for example, the name of a Sunday school class or small group to which they belong, a mission project they support, which worship service they attend, or if they are a visitor. Extend a special welcome to anyone who does not regularly attend your church and invite them to worship at your church if they do not have a church home.

Housekeeping

- Share any necessary information about your meeting space and parking.
- Let participants know you will be faithful to the scheduled meeting time, and encourage everyone to arrive on time.
- Encourage participants to read the upcoming chapter before the next session.

- You may want to invite participants to have a notebook, journal, or electronic tablet for use during this study. Explain that these can be used to record questions and insights they have as they read each chapter and to take notes during each session.
- Ask participants to covenant together to respect a policy of confidentiality within the group.

Leading into the Study

Describe the three types of fishing common in Simon Peter's day: (1) line and hook, (2) casting nets, and (3) dragnet or seine. These are explained in the section of *Simon Peter* titled "Fishermen in the Greco-Roman World" (pages 21–24). Note Hamilton's point that fishermen who fished for a living in the first century usually did dragnet or seine fishing.

Invite volunteers to share their experiences of fishing and note which types of fishing they have done.

Watch your time during this discussion so you will have plenty of time for the Video, Bible Study, Book Study, and/or Optional Activity.

Opening Prayer

Holy God, we thank you for Jesus Christ who calls us to faith in you. We thank you for his disciple Simon Peter who accepted Jesus' call to fish for people. We thank you for the fellowship of this group and the opportunity to learn more about your disciple Simon Peter. Open our hearts to be receptive to your call to fish for people. Open our eyes so that we may see the ways you are calling us to serve you. In the name of your son, Jesus Christ, we pray. Amen.

Learning Together

Video Study and Discussion

Play the DVD, then invite the group to discuss these questions:

- What is one thing you learned about Simon Peter that you did not know before? How did seeing Bethsaida and Capernaum bring Simon's story to life?

- How does it change your perception of Jesus' life and ministry to see some of the places where he taught, healed, and performed miracles?
- Why is it important to hold on to the memory of places like Peter's house? What benefit do people gain from making pilgrimages and visits to such places?
- What other insights or observations did you gain into Peter's story from the video?

Bible Study and Discussion

Read, or invite a volunteer to read, Luke 5:1-5.

> *One day Jesus was standing beside Lake Gennesaret when the crowd pressed in around him to hear God's word. Jesus saw two boats sitting by the lake. The fishermen had gone ashore and were washing their nets. Jesus boarded one of the boats, the one that belonged to Simon, then asked him to row out a little distance from the shore. Jesus sat down and taught the crowds from the boat. When he finished speaking to the crowds, he said to Simon, "Row out farther, into the deep water, and drop your nets for a catch."*
>
> *Simon replied, "Master, we've worked hard all night and caught nothing."*
>
> *(Luke 5:1-5a)*

Note that Lake Gennesaret is another name for the Sea of Galilee. Ask:

- What were the fishermen doing when Jesus spoke to Simon Peter? *(Specifically, they were cleaning their nets after a night of fishing. Make the point that Simon Peter was going about his normal, everyday work when Jesus called him.)*
- What did Jesus first ask Simon Peter to do? *("row out a little distance from the shore")*
- What did Jesus ask Simon Peter to do after he finished teaching the crowds? *("Row out farther, into the deep water, and drop your nets for a catch.")*

Invite participants to consider the difference between shallow water "a little distance from the shore" and "deep water." Ask:

- How do you feel when you are in shallow water?
- How do you feel when you are in deep water?
- What is required of you when you are in shallow water versus when you are in deep water?
- What areas of ministry and service feel like being in "shallow water" for you?
- What areas of ministry and service cause you to feel as if you are in "deep water" or "in over your head"?

Note that "shallow water" and "deep water" are not judgments of the value of a particular area of service, but are used to help participants consider their comfort level with the various ministries Jesus calls us to do. For example, teaching a class may feel like being in shallow water to one person and deep water to another!

Point out that the text does not say Simon Peter protested rowing Jesus out a short distance. He only protested the instruction to row out to the deep water. Ask:

- What reasons did Simon Peter offer for not wanting to go out fishing again? (see verse 5)
- What reasons are you likely to offer for not wanting to respond to a call to serve in what to you feels like "deep water?"

Note to the leader: There will be an opportunity to discuss Simon Peter's remark, "But because you say so" (5:5b) later in the session.

Book Study and Discussion

Invite participants to turn to the introduction in *Simon Peter*. Note Hamilton's observation in the fourth paragraph that all four Gospel writers describe two sides of Simon Peter. We see him "as a flawed disciple—one who seeks to follow Jesus, yet one who is also confused, afraid, and faltering." At the same time, we see "his courage, his determination, his longing to follow Jesus even if it costs him his life" (pages 10–11). Ask:

- Why do you think the Gospel writers included stories that portray Simon Peter's flaws alongside his strengths?
- How does Simon Peter represent "all who seek to follow Jesus"? (page 15).

Geography and Culture around the Sea of Galilee

Share information from the sections in *Simon Peter* titled "The Sea of Galilee," "Simon Bar Jonah," and "Fishermen in the Greco-Roman World" (pages 15–24). Call attention to the maps and photographs in the book. Depending on the time available for your session, you may want to invite participants who have been to the Sea of Galilee and surrounding area to share their observations. Ask:

- In what ways is the name "Simon," which means "to hear" or "to listen," an appropriate name for the disciple Simon Peter? (During the discussion of this question participants may also cite times when Simon Peter did not "hear" or "listen.")
- Who were the *am ha'aretz*?
- How were the *am ha'aretz* different from the Pharisees and other leaders?
- Why do you think Jesus called fisherman who were *am ha'aretz* to be his disciples?

Simon Peter Meets Jesus

Read, or invite a volunteer to read, Luke 3:3. Ask Adam's question:

- "What was it that led these Galilean fishermen, who, it was supposed, were not so religiously devout, to take a week away from their nets and livelihood, traveling four or five days on foot each way, to hear John preaching in the desert?" (page 25).

Read the account of Simon Peter's first encounter with Jesus recorded in John 1:35-42. Note that the name "Cephas" (Aramaic) or "Petros/Peter" (Greek) means "rock." Ask:

- Who introduced Simon Peter to Jesus? *(his brother, Andrew)*
- What qualities did Andrew have that made him an effective evangelist and disciple? *(He worked "behind the scenes" to encourage and help others grow in faith.)*
- What are some reasons why Jesus may have given Simon Peter the nickname "rock"? (Refer to the section in *Simon Peter* titled "From Simon to Peter" for ideas during this discussion.)
- What nicknames describe the way *you see yourself* as a disciple of Christ?
- What nickname would you like Jesus to give you as a sign of the potential he sees in you?
- What talents and skills do you have that Jesus may want to "borrow" for the work of fishing for people? (Invite participants to refer to the section titled "Borrowing Simon's Boat: Our Time, Talent, and Stuff" during the discussion of this question.)

"But because you say so"

Read, or invite a volunteer to read Luke 5:5-11. Call attention to Hamilton's point that Simon Peter only agreed to go fishing again because it was Jesus who suggested it. The text leaves us doubting that Simon Peter would have done so for anyone else.

Call attention to the section in *Simon Peter* titled "Overcoming Our Excuses." Ask:

- What are some of the excuses we offer when we are reluctant to say yes to Jesus' call to serve? (You may want to list these on a board or chart paper.)
- When have you said to Jesus, "But because you say so … I will do it"?
- What happened when you said yes?

If you have a large group, create small teams of three to five people for the discussion of the above three questions so that everyone who would like to share has the opportunity to do so. Let the groups know the time available for this discussion. When you call the groups back together, invite each group to share two or three insights from their discussion.

Share this quote from Hamilton:

> "There are times when Jesus asks us to do things that
> we don't want to do, when we feel tired, or when what
> we're being asked to do seems to make no sense to us. I
> have, on many occasions, been a very *reluctant disciple*.
> For us, the deep water is the place where Jesus calls us
> to go when we'd rather stay on the shore. We feel Christ
> calling and we drag our feet, and sometimes we even say
> no " (page 34).

Then ask:

- What can we do to help us move past our reluctance and excuses so that we may become eager disciples for Jesus Christ?

Optional Activity

Say: Simon Peter was a fisherman. This is the life he knew. His skills and abilities were related to the work of fishing. Then ask:

- How did Simon Peter's background as a fisherman enable him to effectively "fish for people" for Jesus Christ? (Responses may include: he was physically strong, persistent, and accustomed to hard work.)

On a board or chart paper list the various vocations and careers represented by the participants in your group. These will include parent, homemaker, caregiver, volunteer, paid employment, and others. When the list is complete, ask:

- How do the talents and skills required for the vocations and careers on this list enable us to effectively "fish for people" for Jesus Christ?

Wrapping Up

Closing Activity

Fishing For People

Point out that in the closing section of chapter 1, "Fishing for People," Hamilton calls Jesus' invitation to fish for people a movement that is transforming the world. Ask Hamilton's questions (page 39):

- How are you influencing people for Christ?
- How do you represent him by your actions and by your words?

Call attention to Hamilton's comment that "the adventure begins when we say, Yes!…to a mission of fishing for people (page 39). Ask:

- How have you experienced adventure through following Christ?

Share Hamilton's hope for this study found at the end of the introduction: "Ultimately, I hope to help you see yourself in Simon Peter, the flawed but ultimately faithful follower of Jesus Christ" (page 11).

Invite participants to reflect on the following question during the coming week:

- How am I a flawed but faithful disciple of Jesus Christ?

Closing Prayer

Invite participants to pray together the prayer at the end of chapter 1 in *Simon Peter*.

2

WALKING WITH JESUS IN THE STORMS

Planning the Session

Session Goals

Through conversation, activities, and reflection, participants will:

- consider Simon Peter's experience of walking on the water toward Jesus,
- examine their own experiences of facing "storms" in their lives,
- and affirm Jesus' continuing presence through all the "storms" we face.

Biblical Foundation

Matthew 14:22-34

Before the Session

- Set up a table in the room with name tags, markers, Bibles, and extra copies of *Simon Peter* if these will be needed.

- Have a whiteboard or chart paper and markers or a chalkboard and chalk available for recording participants' responses.
- On a board or large sheet of paper write the heading "Storms." Below the heading draw a vertical line to make two columns. Label the first column "Characteristics" and the second column "Feelings."
- Write the three phrases Jesus spoke in Matthew 14:27 in a column on a board or large sheet of paper. This will be used in the discussion of "Stepping Out of the Boat."
  ◊ "Be encouraged!"
  ◊ "It's me."
  ◊ "Don't be afraid."
- Read the instructions for the two Optional Activities near the end of the lesson plan.
  ◊ If you want to do the optional music activity, collect hymnals and worship songbooks. You may also want to recruit an accompanist.
  ◊ If you want to do the optional art activity, collect paper and crayons, markers, and/or colored pencils. Additional ideas for art supplies are listed with the instructions for this activity. Your church's children's minister may help you locate these.
  ◊ You may offer both of these Optional Activities at the same time and give participants a choice of which they would like to do.

Getting Started

Opening Activities

Greet participants as they arrive. If there are newcomers allow a short time for introductions.

Share any housekeeping items that need repeating. (See the list for session 1.) Remind participants to respect a policy of confidentiality within the group.

Leading into the Study

Say: We have all (probably) experienced rainstorms complete with thunder and lightning. Some of us have experienced other storms in the natural world like hurricanes and tornadoes.

Call attention to the board or chart paper with the heading "Storms" and the columns labeled "Characteristics" and "Feelings." Record responses in the appropriate column during the discussion of the following questions. Ask:

- What are the characteristics of these storms?
- What feelings have you experienced during these storms?

Opening Prayer

Holy God, Lord of all creation, we thank you for the world you have made. We confess that we grow fearful in the midst of storms. We thank you for your continuing presence with us. Thank you for the people in this group and for this time to study your word together. Thank you for your disciple Simon Peter who shows us that we, too, may be faithful disciples, in spite of our flaws. Guide and bless our time together. Help us to remember you are always with us through the storms we face. In Jesus' name we pray, Amen.

Learning Together

Video Study and Discussion

Play the DVD, then invite the group to discuss the following questions:

- What might it mean that so much of Jesus' time with the disciples was spent on or around the water?
- Recall the archaeological artifact known as the "Jesus boat." How likely is it that this boat was actually used by Jesus and his disciples? (*Not very likely, though a similar one may have been.*)
- What is the value of finds like this to our faith, even if they are not directly connected to Jesus or the disciples?

- Does seeing these places make you feel closer to Jesus? Why or why not?
- What new insights or questions about Peter's life do you have after seeing the video?

Bible Study and Discussion

Read or invite a volunteer to read Matthew 14:22-24.

Right then, Jesus made the disciples get into the boat and go ahead to the other side of the lake while he dismissed the crowds. When he sent them away, he went up onto a mountain by himself to pray. Evening came and he was alone. Meanwhile, the boat, fighting a strong headwind, was being battered by the waves and was already far away from land.

Invite participants to turn to Matthew 14 in their Bibles. Explain that the story of "walking on the water" takes place after two other significant events in Jesus' life: the "Death of John the Baptist" recorded in Matthew 14:1-12 and the "Feeding the five thousand" recorded in Matthew 14:13-21. (Story titles are from the CEB.) Remind the group that John the Baptist was Jesus' cousin.

Read Matthew 14:12-13. Ask:

- What did Jesus do when he learned his cousin had died?
- Why do you think he did this? *(Possibly to grieve the death of his cousin)*
- Who interrupted Jesus' time alone?
- How did Jesus respond to the crowds? *(with compassion)*
- How do you think Jesus felt after he performed the miracles of healing and feeding the crowd? *(Perhaps he was weary and still grieving his cousin's death)*

Read again Matthew 14:22-24. Ask:

- What "storms" were Jesus and the disciples experiencing at this time? *(Jesus perhaps storms of grief and weariness, the disciples a physical storm at sea)*

- Why was this time of prayer and solitude important for Jesus?
- What does this teach us about our own need for times of solitude and prayer with God? (*Through prayer we find healing from "storms" we have experienced in the past, strength to weather the storms we are currently facing, and courage to move ahead in faith.*)

Book Study and Discussion

The Sea—A Place of Fear

Describe the Sea of Galilee and the boats that were common in Jesus' day, using the section titled "Jesus' Boat" as a guide (pages 43–45).

Point out that the people were afraid of the sea. One of the reasons for this was that they could not measure its depth. This led to the belief that it was endless and opened to the underworld, which was "the realm of the dead" (page 47).

The sea was also home to the sea monster Leviathan.

Generally speaking, the sea was a dangerous and mysterious place, often identified with malevolent forces in ancient Near Eastern thought.

Read Matthew 14:25-26. Remind the group that the disciples were in the midst of experiencing a raging storm at sea. Ask:

- Why did the disciples jump to the conclusion that the person they saw walking on the water was a ghost? (*They believed the entrance to the underworld, the place of the dead, was beneath them at the bottom of the sea.*)
- How did the disciples express their terror at seeing a "ghost?" (*Screaming*)
- Where are the "seas" or places of fear in your life?
- What storms have you faced that caused you to feel frightened, even terrified to the point of screaming?

If you have a large group, you may want to invite participants to share responses to the last two questions above in smaller groups of from two to four people. Remind the group of the agreement to respect confidentiality.

Stepping Out of the Boat

Read Matthew 14:27-32.

Emphasize Hamilton's point that Jesus was watching over his disciples during their time of need even when they were not aware of it. (See the section titled "A Storm on the Sea," pages 45–49.) Ask:

- What did Jesus say to comfort his disciples? (see verse 27) Call attention to the board or paper with these phrases as described in "Before the Session."
  ◊ "Be encouraged!"
  ◊ "It's me."
  ◊ "Don't be afraid."
- When have you heard Jesus say these phrases to you?
- How has the knowledge of Jesus' encouragement and presence helped you move past your fear?
- What did Jesus do about calming the actual storm before he reached the boat? *(Nothing!)*
- Why do you think Simon Peter wanted to leave the relative safety of the boat to come to Jesus? (Invite participants to turn to the section of chapter 2 titled "Lord, Command Me to Come to You" during the discussion of this question.)

Suggest that Simon Peter deserves a lot of credit for getting out of the boat in the first place. It takes courage for a person to step out of one's comfort zone, no matter what that comfort zone may be. Remind the group of the discussion about "shallow water" and "deep water" during the last session. The point was made that an area of service that feels like being in "shallow water" for one person may feel like being in "deep water" to another person. Likewise, what is a baby step of faith for one person may be a leap of faith for another. With that in mind, ask:

- What happened after Simon Peter stepped out of the boat? During the discussion of verses 30 to 32 be sure the following points are mentioned:

◊ Simon Peter's first response after he became frightened was to call out to Jesus with faith, believing that Jesus could and would help him. Simon Peter did not give up and turn away.

◊ When Simon Peter called out "Lord, rescue me!" (verse 30), Jesus' response was immediate. Jesus "immediately reached out and grabbed" (verse 31) Simon Peter.

◊ Jesus' comment "You man of weak faith! Why did you begin to have doubts?" sounds like a reprimand but may have been an expression of disappointment. Share Hamilton's insight about this in the section titled "Rescue Me" in chapter 2 (pages 53–54).

◊ Jesus did not calm the storm at that point. He walked with Simon Peter through the storm.

Ask:

- Why do you think Jesus waited until he and Simon Peter were in the boat before he calmed the storm?
- Have you ever stepped out in faith and then found yourself "sinking" with fear? If yes, what did you do?
- How have you experienced Jesus walking with you through frightening and challenging times?

The Sea—A Place to Experience God's Love

Read, or invite a volunteer to read, Psalm 107:23-32. Note Hamilton's comment that this is "thought to be the psalm of the sailors" (page 55). Ask:

- What does this psalm tell us about the sailors' experience on the sea?
- What does it tell us about God's actions on behalf of the sailors?
- What does it say about the sailors' response to God's intervention and love?

Read Matthew 14:32-33. Ask:

- How did Jesus' disciples respond after "the wind settled down" (verses 32-33)? (Invite the group to refer to the section in chapter 2 titled "Who Is This Man?" on pages 54–56 for input during this discussion.)
- How does their response compare to that of the sailors when "God quieted the storm to a whisper" (Psalm 107:29)?
- How have you responded to God when he has walked with you and/or calmed the storms in your life?

Optional Activities

Music

Hamilton mentions Thomas Dorsey and his hymn "Precious Lord, Take My Hand" (*The United Methodist Hymnal*, 474). Another hymn that is relevant to Matthew 14:22-34 is "Stand By Me" (*UMH*, 512).

Provide hymnals and worship songbooks and suggest that participants with electronic devices may search the Internet during this activity. You may also want to recruit a pianist ahead of time to accompany the hymns and songs. If the pianist is not a participant in your group, share with him or her the agreement to respect confidentiality within the group. Let participants know they may work as a group, in pairs, or alone.

Instruct participants to:

- Read Matthew 14:22-34.
- Find hymns and songs that reflect the themes present in this Scripture passage.
- Sing or say the words to the hymns together, or listen to recordings you may find on the Internet.

Art

In Matthew 14:22-34, the Gospel writer describes several scenes including:

- The frightened disciples enduring a storm at sea
- Jesus and Simon Peter walking on the water
- The disciples worshiping Jesus after Jesus calms the storm.

Provide paper in two sizes so participants will have a choice of 8 1/2-by-11 inches or larger pieces of chart paper. Provide a variety of crayons, markers, and/or colored pencils. You may have ideas for other art supplies you would like to provide—perhaps paper in various colors, as well as pieces of yarn, cloth, or ribbon for making a collage. If you provide materials for making a collage you will also need scissors and glue or tape.

Let participants know that they may work alone or in small groups of from two to four people, and also how much time is available for this activity.

Note that the "finished product" will likely be an "abstract" and that there is no "wrong" way to do this activity.

Instruct participants to:

- Read Matthew 14:22-34.
- Draw a vertical line in the middle of the piece of paper.
- On the left side of the paper depict your feelings when you are in the midst of a storm. The storm may be an actual thunderstorm or an internal emotional or spiritual storm. The storm the person has in mind does not need to be revealed.
- On the right side of the paper depict your feelings after God has seen you through the storm.
- At the end of the time invite volunteers to share their work.

Please note: You may want to offer both the music activity and the art activity at the same time and invite participants to choose the one they would like to do. Let participants know how much time is available for the groups to work on these projects. Then offer a time for volunteers to share their work.

Wrapping Up

Closing Activity

Remind the group of the title of chapter 2, "Walking with Jesus in the Storms."

Invite discussion of this question:

- How has this study of Matthew 14:22-34 helped you grow to be a more faithful disciple of Jesus Christ?

Closing Prayer

Pray together the prayer at the end of chapter 2 in *Simon Peter*.

3

BEDROCK OR STUMBLING BLOCK?

Planning the Session

Session Goals

Through conversation, activities, and reflection, participants will:

- affirm the meaning of Simon Peter's confession of faith, "You are the Christ, the Son of the living God;"
- realize the significance of Simon Peter's call to be the rock on which Jesus built his church;
- and consider the differences between God's thoughts and ways and human thoughts and ways.

Biblical Foundation

Matthew 16:13-23, selected verses

Before the Session

- Set up a table in the room with name tags, markers, Bibles, and extra copies of *Simon Peter* if these will be needed.

- Have a whiteboard or chart paper and markers or a chalkboard and chalk available for recording participants' responses.
- Write the heading "Who is Jesus?" at the top of a board or large sheet of paper. This will be used in the "Leading into the Study" activity.
- On another board or large sheet of paper write the heading "Caesarea Philippi." This will be used in the Book Study discussion of "Why This Place?"
- Read the Optional Activity and decide if you want to include this in your lesson plan.

Getting Started

Opening Activities

Greet participants as they arrive. If there are newcomers allow a short time for introductions.

Share any housekeeping items that need repeating. (See the list from session 1.) Remind participants to respect a policy of confidentiality within the group.

Leading into the Study

Call attention to the board or large sheet of paper with the heading "Who is Jesus?"

Offer these instructions:

- Call out one-word and two-word answers to the question "Who is Jesus?"
- Do not think about your answers. Call out the first ideas that come to mind.
- We have three minutes for this activity.

Recruit a volunteer to watch the time. Write responses on the board or large sheet of paper. These responses will be reviewed during the Bible Study and Discussion

Opening Prayer

Holy God, we thank you for sending Jesus to show us the way to you. We thank you for Simon Peter who answered your call to be the rock upon which you built your church. Open our eyes to the work you call us to do and give us the courage to say yes. We know that as you were able to use Simon Peter, flaws and all, you are able to work through us to make disciples for Jesus Christ. Amen.

Learning Together

Video Study and Discussion

Play the DVD, then invite the group to discuss the following questions:

- How did you feel viewing the scenery at Caesarea Philippi? How do you think the disciples would have felt surrounded by such natural beauty as well as shrines to other gods?
- How does this setting shape your understanding of the importance of Simon Peter's declaration that Jesus is "the Christ, the Son of the Living God"?
- The location of the mountain where Jesus was transfigured is unknown, but some parts of the Christian tradition identify it as Mount Tabor. What insights into Jesus' identity did Peter gain on the mountain when Jesus was transfigured?
- What new observations or questions do you have after viewing the video?

Following the video, invite volunteers to share their responses to the questions above.

Bible Study and Discussion

Read, or invite a volunteer to read, Matthew 16:15-16.

> He said, "And what about you? Who do you say that I am?"

> Simon Peter said, "You are the Christ, the Son of the living God."

The focus of this discussion is the meaning of Simon Peter's identification of Jesus as "the Christ, the Son of the living God."

Note that this conversation took place before the death and resurrection of Jesus. Therefore, as Hamilton points out (page 65), it does not represent everything that Christians have come to believe about Jesus. Review the responses from the "Leading into the Study" activity for the question "Who is Jesus?" and note that these responses represent what twenty-first-century Christians in the group believe about Jesus.

Call attention to the words *Christos* and *Messiah* and share these points:

- *Christos* is Greek. The New Testament was written in Greek.
- *Messiah* is Hebrew, the language of the Old Testament.
- The literal translation of these two words is "anointed one."
- In biblical times, both people and objects were anointed with oil.
- Priests and kings were anointed to show they were chosen by God to serve God's people, both as religious leaders and political leaders.
- Objects were anointed to indicate their sacred place in the Tabernacle and Temple.
- Old Testament prophets called the people to look for and hope for "the ideal king...*the* Anointed One" (page 66).

Invite participants to refer to the sections titled "You Are the Messiah" and "You Are the Son of God" as they answer these questions (pages 65–67). Ask:

- Who or what did the Jews expect the "Anointed One" to be?
- In what ways did Jesus fulfill this expectation?
- In what ways did Jesus not fulfill this expectation?
- Why do you think Simon Peter spoke up and made his statement of faith?

Book Study and Discussion

Why This Place?

Read Matthew 16:13 and Mark 8:27. Ask:

- Where did this conversation between Jesus and his disciples take place?
- What do we know about this area? (Invite participants to scan chapter 3 for this information and record responses on the board or large sheet of paper with the heading "Caesarea Philippi." Mention the following key points if they are not offered by the group.)
  - ◊ It was a remote area, twenty-five miles north of the Sea of Galilee, at the base of Mount Hermon.
  - ◊ It is an area noted for its beauty and is presently called the Hermon Stream Nature Reserve.
  - ◊ It was predominantly a non-Jewish area.
  - ◊ The area was used for the worship of pagan deities.
  - ◊ There is a waterfall there. (Invite a volunteer to read the fourth paragraph in the opening section of chapter 3 for a description of the waterfall.)
  - ◊ The chasm there was believed by some to be an entrance to the underworld or Hades. (Recall that in chapter 2 it was noted that the Sea of Galilee was also believed to be an entrance to this realm of the dead.)
- Why is the area called "Caesarea Philippi"?

Call attention to Hamilton's suggestion that Jesus intentionally chose this location for this conversation with his disciples. As the disciples gathered around Jesus, the shrines to a pagan god and an oppressive Roman ruler were in sight. Jesus affirms Simon Peter's proclamation that he is "the Christ, the Son of the living God." In other words, Jesus is the long-awaited Messiah. Ask:

- What is the significance of the phrase "living God"? (*Only God is "the living God." The pagan god honored in the nearby shrine had no life and therefore no power to influence the lives of humankind.*)

- What expectations did the Jews have regarding Jesus' actions toward oppressive Roman rulers like the one honored in the nearby shrine?
- How do you think the disciples were feeling at this moment?
- What thoughts may have been running through their minds?

Peter the Rock

Read, or invite a volunteer to read, Matthew 16:17-20. Note these two key points:

- Simon Peter will have a leading role in the development of the Christian community.
- Christ's church will be stronger than "The gates of the underworld" (verse 18).

Ask:

- What authority did Jesus give Simon Peter in the establishment of his church? (See the section titled "The Gates of Hades" on pages 72–74 for information to guide this discussion.)

Call attention to Jesus' words to Simon Peter in verse 17, "Happy are you, Simon son of Jonah, because no human has shown this to you. Rather my Father who is in heaven has shown you." Note that the NRSV and NIV translate "Blessed" in place of "Happy." Ask:

- How do you think Simon Peter was feeling at this point in the story, in light of the fact that:
  ◊ He is in the presence of the promised Messiah or Christ,
  ◊ Jesus has just called him "Happy" and "Blessed," and
  ◊ Jesus has given him authority over the building of his church?
- (Responses may include excited, joyful, honored, nervous, and overwhelmed.)

"Get behind me, Satan"

In the discussion of "Peter the Rock" above, we noted that Simon Peter was likely feeling positive about things. These feelings quickly changed when Jesus foretold what the future held for their Messiah. Read Matthew 16:21-23. Ask:

- What did Simon Peter say to Jesus after Jesus foretold his coming suffering and death? (*"God forbid, Lord! This won't happen to you,"* verse 22.)
- How do you think Simon Peter felt at this point in the story? (Note that Simon Peter seems not to have heard Jesus' prediction of his resurrection.)
- What are the differences between "God's thoughts" and "human thoughts" in verse 23?

Read Isaiah 55:8-9:

> *My plans aren't your plans,*
> *nor are your ways my ways, says the LORD.*
> *Just as the heavens are higher than the earth,*
> *so are my ways higher than your ways,*
> *and my plans than your plans.*

Read Matthew 4:1-11, the story of Jesus' temptation in the wilderness. Ask:

- What were the three temptations that Satan or "the tempter" presented to Jesus?
  - ◊ To satisfy his physical needs and "command these stones to become bread" (verse 3)
  - ◊ To test God by throwing himself off of "the highest point of the temple" (verse 5)
  - ◊ To worship Satan instead of God.
- What Scripture passages did Jesus quote as he resisted each of these three temptations? (See Matthew 4:4, 7, 10.)

- What two similar phrases did Jesus speak in Matthew 4 to Satan and in Matthew 16 to Simon Peter? ("Go away, Satan," Matthew 4:10, and "Get behind me, Satan," Matthew 16:23).
- What did Jesus mean when he said the words in verse 23 to Simon Peter?
- How might Simon Peter be a stone that would cause Jesus to "stumble"?

You may wish to do the Optional Activity "Get Behind Me, Satan" following this discussion.

Optional Activity

"Get behind me, Satan"

The purpose of this activity is to encourage participants to consider how various temptations keep us from following God's will for our lives. We need to follow Jesus' example and command those people and things that are drawing us away from God to "get behind us."

Invite participants to form small groups of from four to six people. Offer these instructions:

- Create a short play to present to the group based on the story of Jesus' temptation in the wilderness (Matthew 4:1-11).
- The play should be a *present-day scenario* based on one of the temptations Jesus faced.
- The short play may be presented as silent acting with a narrator, actors/actresses with speaking parts, or a combination of these.
- End the play with Jesus' words, "Go away, Satan" (Matthew 4:10) or "Get behind me, Satan" (Matthew 16:23).

Let participants know how much time they will have to create the play and how much time they will have to present the play so that all groups may "perform."

Wrapping Up

Closing Activity

Recall the title of chapter 3, "Bedrock or Stumbling Block?" Ask:

- Who or what have been "bedrocks" for you in your faith journey?
- Who or what have been "stumbling blocks" for you in your faith journey?
- In what ways have you been "bedrock" for others as they have grown in faith in Christ?

Closing Prayer

Pray the prayer at the end of chapter 3 in *Simon Peter* together.

4

"I WILL NOT DENY YOU"

Planning the Session

Session Goals

Through conversation, activities, and reflection, participants will:

- privately confess a time when he or she denied knowing Jesus, then accepted God's forgiveness;
- consider the impact of servant leadership in our world today;
- and discover ways that our confession of our flaws may inspire others to faith in Christ.

Biblical Foundation

Matthew 26:31-35 NRSV

Before the Session

- Set up a table in the room with name tags, markers, Bibles, and extra copies of *Simon Peter* if these will be needed.
- Have a whiteboard or chart paper and markers, or a chalkboard and chalk, available for recording participants' responses.

- In preparation for the "Leading into the Study" activity:
  - ◊ Provide a piece of paper (notebook or printer paper), a pencil, and a plain white envelope (either letter or legal size) for each participant.
  - ◊ Place a basket large enough to hold all the participants' envelopes on a table in a prominent place in your meeting space.
  - ◊ You may want to print the questions listed with the "Leading into the Study" activity at the top of each participant's piece of paper, or write them on a board or large sheet of paper and display it in the room.
- For the "Bible Study and Discussion," review the three options for how to lead the discussion of the last two questions.
- If you want to do the "Optional Activity," write this quote from chapter 4 of *Simon Peter* on a board or large sheet of paper: "Jesus is the Lord of the second chance" (page 105).

Getting Started

Opening Activities

Greet participants as they arrive. If there are newcomers allow a short time for introductions.

Share any housekeeping items that need repeating. (See the list from session 1.) Remind participants to respect a policy of confidentiality within the group.

Leading into the Study

Read the Scripture passage for this lesson, Matthew 26:31-35.

Distribute a piece of paper, a pencil, and an envelope to each participant. Assure participants that what they write on their piece of paper will remain confidential. No one will read it. Offer these instructions:

- Write your response to one of the following on your piece of paper.
  - ◊ When was a time you denied knowing Jesus? Why?
  - ◊ When was a time you deserted someone who needed your help? What happened?
  - ◊ When was a time you missed an opportunity to serve Christ?
- Fold the paper and place it in the envelope, seal the envelope, and write your name on the front.
- Put your sealed envelope in the basket. You will receive your envelope back at the end of the session.

Remind participants that no one will read what they wrote. When everyone has finished, offer the opening prayer.

Opening Prayer

Loving and forgiving God, we come before you with repentant and thankful hearts. We know that we are like your disciple Simon Peter, both flawed and faithful. Forgive us for the times we turn away from you, the times we deny you, the times we fail to serve others in your name. Thank you for your never-ending love and your grace-filled forgiveness. We look to you for courage and strength, for guidance and direction, as we continue to be your faithful, yet flawed, disciples. Amen.

Learning Together

Video Study and Discussion

Play the DVD, then invite the group to discuss one or more of the following questions:

- In the video we saw two possible locations of the upper room where Jesus washed the disciples' feet. What does Peter's reaction to Jesus washing Peter's feet tell you about him?
- How do you think Simon Peter felt when he was following those who arrested Jesus from Gethsemane to the high priest's house?

- The Church of St. Peter in Gallicantu remembers Jesus' trial, but it's named after Peter's denial of Jesus. Why is it important for the church to remember Peter's denial and commemorate it in this way?
- How does seeing the places in the video bring you new insights into Simon Peter's life and the story of Jesus' arrest and trial? What new questions do you have?

Invite the group members to keep the video in mind as you discuss the Bible and the study book in the rest of your session.

Bible Study and Discussion

Read Matthew 26:26-35. Explain that in verse 31 Jesus is quoting the Old Testament prophet Zechariah. Share the following information about Zechariah and this verse:

- The prophecies in the book of Zechariah concern Israel's future after the Babylonian exile.
- The prophecies offer hope for the restoration of God's people, as indicated in Zechariah 13:1:

> *On that day, a fountain will open*
> *to cleanse the sin and impurity of David's house and the*
> *inhabitants of Jerusalem.*

- The prophecies may be interpreted as eschatological in nature in that they point to the end times.
- Zechariah 13:7, the verse Jesus refers to, says,

> *Sword, arise against my shepherd,*
> *against the man responsible for my community, says the*
> *LORD of heavenly forces!*
> *Strike the shepherd in order to scatter the flock!*

- Jesus is identifying himself as the "shepherd" in Zechariah 13:7. His reference to this verse in Matthew 26:31 foreshadows what

43

is about to take place in the garden where Jesus and his "flock" of disciples are gathered.

Remind the group that Jesus has told the disciples about his upcoming suffering, death, and resurrection on two previous occasions. These are recorded in Matthew 16:21-23 (part of the biblical text for chapter 3) and Matthew 17:22-23. Invite volunteers to read these two Scripture passages.

Note that on the night of his last supper with his disciples, Jesus makes two references to his resurrection. Invite participants to scan Matthew 26 to find these two references (verses 29 and 32). Ask:

- How did the disciples respond when Jesus mentioned his death and resurrection?
- What do you think the disciples were feeling and thinking at this time?

Book Study and Discussion

Washing Feet and True Greatness

Review the events that took place between Jesus' transfiguration and his last supper with his disciples using information presented in the section titled "From Transfiguration to the Upper Room" in chapter 4.

Read John 13:1-20. Point out that John is the only Gospel that includes the story of Jesus washing the disciples' feet. The story of Jesus sharing the bread and cup with his disciples at the Last Supper is recorded in the three Synoptic Gospels—Matthew, Mark, and Luke—but not in John.

Note Hamilton's observation that foot washing is "not a routine task in our culture" (page 94), but it was a common practice in the culture in which Jesus lived. For Jesus' disciples then, Jesus' act of washing their feet was a powerful example of "servant leadership." Ask:

- What is "servant leadership"? (Invite participants to refer to the section titled "Washing Feet and True Greatness" on pages 91–95 during this discussion.)

- What are examples of "servant leadership" in our culture?
- When have you taken on the role of a "servant" toward others?
- How did you feel, or do you feel, when you take on the role of servant?
- When have others taken on the role of servant in their relationship with you?
- How do you feel when you are on the receiving end of someone's act of service? (You may want to invite discussion of Peter's reaction when Jesus washed his feet.)

Invite discussion of Hamilton's last sentence in the section titled "Washing Feet and True Greatness":

> "I wonder how our lives might change if we each saw this as our mission—that we are servants of others, servants of our mates, servants of our customers, servants of our fellow employees, and servants of the servants of God" (page 95).

"I will not deny you."

Reread Peter's declaration in Matthew 26:35 (NRSV). Ask:

- What events took place between the time of Peter's declaration that he would not deny Jesus, and Peter's denial of Jesus in the courtyard? (Invite participants to consult Matthew 26:36-68. As the various events are mentioned you may want to write them in chronological order on a board or large sheet of paper.)
- What led Peter to make such a bold declaration?
- How do you think Peter felt when Jesus predicted that he would deny him?

Confessing Failures

Remind participants of Hamilton's view that Peter's flaws as a disciple are recorded and preserved in the New Testament because Peter himself confessed these failures in his sermons to the early church.

- Hold up the basket of envelopes from the "Leading into the Study" activity. Say:
  - ◊ We, like Peter, are flawed disciples.
  - ◊ We, like Peter, have missed opportunities to witness to our faith and serve others in the name of Christ.
  - ◊ The good news of the gospel is that we, like Peter, are forgiven.
  - ◊ Christ continues to call us to serve others in his name.
- Return the envelopes, unopened, to each participant.
- Read this paragraph from page 105:

"Peter's story also shows us that we need not be defined by our failures. God does not define us by the worst thing we ever did. Jesus makes amazing use of flawed disciples. He continually invites us back, forgives us, and restores us. Sometimes he uses us even more profoundly, not merely in spite of our flaws and failures but because of them. Jesus is the Lord of the second chance. If the disciple who denied knowing Jesus could become the Rock on which the church was built, there is hope for us too. Simon Peter wasn't afraid to talk about his shortcomings as a way to help others learn, grow, and find grace. He knew that every person who commits to follow Jesus would fall short."

- Offer this prayer:

Loving and forgiving God, we are sorry for the times we have denied that we know you and we ask for your forgiveness. We thank you for your forgiveness and your amazing love for us. Open our eyes to the new opportunities you place before us to serve others in the name of Christ. Amen.

Optional Activity

Second Chances

Write this sentence on a board or large sheet of paper: "Jesus is the Lord of the second chance." (This sentence is taken from the section titled "Inspiring Followers by Confessing Failures," page 105.)

If you have a large group, create smaller groups of from four to six people for this activity. Instruct each group to respond to these questions:

- When has God given you a second chance (or multiple chances) to be a faithful disciple?
- Who in your community needs a second chance? (Explain that responses may include a group of people, for example, the homeless; or individuals, for example, a person who has recently returned from prison.)
- What are you or your church currently doing to offer second chances to these groups and/or individuals?
- What can you personally do to share the life-giving news that "Jesus is the Lord of the second chance"?

Wrapping Up

Closing Activity

Share the story of Jorge Acevedo as told in the section titled "Inspiring Followers by Confessing Failures" in chapter 4. Then invite participants to share similar stories. You may want to ask the following questions to help start the conversation:

- How has your confession of your failures and your acceptance of God's forgiveness helped you grow to be a stronger disciple of Christ?
- When have you shared stories of your flaws and God's forgiveness with others?

Closing Prayer

Pray the prayer at the end of *Simon Peter* chapter 4 together.

5

FROM COWARDICE TO COURAGE

Planning the Session

Session Goals

Through conversation, activities, and reflection, participants will:

- consider Simon Peter's feelings and actions between the time he denied knowing Jesus and his experience of receiving Jesus' forgiveness and commission,
- explore the meaning of repentance and forgiveness,
- and discover ways to demonstrate love for Jesus.

Biblical Foundation

John 21:12, 15-17

Before the Session

- Set up a table in the room with name tags, markers, Bibles, and extra copies of *Simon Peter* if these will be needed.
- Have a whiteboard or chart paper and markers or a chalkboard and chalk available for recording participants' responses.

- On a board or large sheet of paper draw three vertical lines to make four columns. Label the first column "Matthew," the second column "Mark," the third column "Luke," and the fourth column "John." This will be used during the discussion titled "Resurrection Morning and Appearances."
- If you choose to do the Optional Activity, make two columns on a board or large sheet of paper. In the first column write the heading "Groups" and in the second column write "Individuals."

Getting Started

Opening Activities

Greet participants as they arrive. If there are newcomers allow a short time for introductions.

Share any housekeeping items that need repeating. (See the list for session 1.) Remind participants to respect a policy of confidentiality within the group.

Leading into the Study

Read John 18:15-18, 25-27. Share these points:

- This is John's account of Simon Peter's denial of Jesus.
- In session 4 we looked at Jesus' prediction of Peter's denial and the events following it (Matthew 26:31-68).
- Matthew's account reports that after denying Jesus, "Peter went out and cried uncontrollably" (Matthew 26:75).
- John's account does not say what Simon Peter did after he heard the rooster crow. He is not mentioned in John's Gospel again until the morning of the Resurrection, John 20:2.

Invite participants to share thoughts as to Simon Peter's actions and feelings between the time he heard the rooster crow and the moment he heard the news of Jesus' resurrection—a time extending from Thursday evening to Sunday morning. Hamilton offers ideas in the opening section of chapter 5. You may want to ask these questions as part of the discussion:

- Do you think Peter ventured to the place of Jesus' crucifixion and watched, unnoticed?
- What do you think you would have done if you were in Simon Peter's position?

Opening Prayer

Holy and forgiving God, we want to be your faithful disciples, but sometimes, like Simon Peter, we stumble and we deny that we even know you. We come before you with repentant hearts and ask for your forgiveness. We find hope in the knowledge that you forgave your disciple Simon Peter. We trust you will forgive us. We pray that you will give us courage and strength, so that we, like Simon Peter, may be your faithful disciples and share the good news of Jesus Christ. Amen.

Learning Together

Video Study and Discussion

Play the DVD, then invite the group to discuss the following questions:

- What parts of the Church of the Holy Sepulcher resonated with you the most? How might the church's memory of Jesus' death and burial at this place strengthen the faith of those who visit?
- Adam Hamilton notes that Peter and some of the other disciples went back to Galilee to resume fishing after Jesus' death and resurrection. Why might they have done that? How did their encounter with the risen Jesus by the lakeshore affect Peter?
- Why was it important for Jesus to ask Peter "Do you love me?" three times? What hope do you gain from the scene of Peter's reinstatement?
- What new observations or questions do you have after viewing the video?

Invite the group members to keep the video in mind as you discuss the Bible and the study book in the rest of your session.

Bible Study and Discussion

Invite a volunteer to read Luke 5:1-11. This is the text for chapter 1 in *Simon Peter* and is printed in the book.

Invite another volunteer to read John 21:1-14. This text precedes the focal text for this session. Ask:

- What are the similarities between these two stories?

Book Study and Discussion

Resurrection Morning and Appearances

Call attention to the fact that there are both similarities and differences in the four Gospel accounts of Easter morning and Jesus' resurrection appearances to his disciples.

Invite participants to count off by four and to remember their number. It is not necessary for participants to move and sit with their group. Assign Scripture passages as below.

- Ones: Matthew 28:1-10, 16-20
- Twos: Mark 16:1-7 (Explain that there are alternate endings for the Gospel of Mark. For the purposes of this session we will only look at Mark 16:1-7.)
- Threes: Luke 24:1-53
- Fours: John 20:1-31 (Explain that John 21 will be discussed later in the session.)

Offer a few minutes for participants to skim their assigned Scripture text. Then ask the questions below. After *each* question, invite those who read Matthew to answer first, then those who read Mark, then those who read Luke, ending with the ones who read John. Record the responses in the appropriate column on the board or large sheet of paper (this is explained in Before the Session). Ask:

1. Who discovered the empty tomb on Easter morning?
2. When did she/they go to the tomb?

3. Who did she/they encounter at the tomb?
4. What was she/were they instructed to do and by whom?
5. To whom did Jesus appear after his resurrection?
6. What does this text tell us about Peter?
7. Where are the similarities between these four Gospel accounts? Circle these.
8. Where are the differences between these four Gospel accounts?

As you conclude the discussion of questions 7 and 8, note that all four Gospels agree on the most important points!

Call attention to the angel's instruction in Mark 16:7 to "Go, tell his disciples, especially Peter" and also the section in chapter 5 titled "Especially Peter." Remind the group that Mark is the oldest of the four Gospels. Ask:

• Why do you think the angel added the phrase "especially Peter"?

A Charcoal Fire

Remind the group of the discussion of John 21:1-14 (Leading into the Study) and note that these verses set the scene for the Biblical Foundation text for this session. Invite a volunteer to read John 21:15-17. Ask:

• What is the significance of the charcoal fire? (Contribute information about the charcoal fire found in the section titled "Peter, Do You Love Me?" on pages 120–124 of chapter 5 during this discussion.)
• Why did Jesus ask Simon Peter his question "do you love me" three times? (This corresponds to Simon Peter denying Jesus three times.)
• What did Jesus ask Simon Peter to do? (Note that Jesus' call is worded three ways but all three ways carry the same meaning.)
• Why was this experience so important to Simon Peter and also to Christ's church?

Call attention to the fact that the meal Jesus prepared over the charcoal fire, bread and fish, was reminiscent of the last supper Jesus shared with his disciples before his crucifixion and resurrection. Since that time Christians around the world have observed the breaking of bread as a symbol of Communion with Christ.

Share this quote by Adam Hamilton from *Simon Peter* on page 120:

> "The Eucharist, Lord's Supper, Holy Communion,
> whatever you call this meal, is a meal aimed not only at
> remembering and connecting us with Christ and one
> another as his disciples, it is also a meal of reconciliation
> and forgiveness. This meal at the shoreline was all of these
> things for Simon Peter."

Share the invitation from the United Methodist Liturgy for Holy Communion:

> "Christ our Lord invites to his table all who love him,
>   who earnestly repent of their sin
>   and seek to live in peace with one another.
> Therefore, let us confess our sin before God and one another."[1]

Ask:

- What does this invitation ask of us?
- Why is our repentance of sin so important for our relationship with Christ?
- In what ways have you experienced God's forgiveness?
- How has your acceptance of God's forgiveness given you the freedom to serve wholeheartedly as a disciple of Christ?
- When have you felt Christ's presence in the breaking of bread?

Offer a time for participants to ask questions and share new insights related to John 21:15-17 and the section in chapter 5 titled "Peter, Do You Love Me?"

---

1   From Invitation of *The United Methodist Hymnal*, 1989. Copyright 1989 by The United Methodist Publishng House; "A Service of Word and Table I"; page 7. Used by permission.

Optional Activity

Love in Action

Jesus continues to call disciples to care for others. The text from Matthew 25:34-40 suggests specific ways to do this. Invite a volunteer to read the text.

Explain that "the king" or the speaker in this story is Jesus. Jesus told this story two days before his last supper with his disciples (Matthew 26: 1-2). Ask:

- What specific acts of service are mentioned in this story? (*feed the hungry, give a drink to the thirsty, welcome the stranger, clothe the naked, care for the sick, visit the ones in prison*)
- What ministries are in place through our church and community to serve Christ in these ways? (Responses may include local food banks and co-ops, Kairos or other prison ministries, and health clinics. Record responses on the board or large sheet of paper under the heading "Group.")
- In what ways do you as an individual serve Christ in these ways? (Responses may include contributing food to a food bank, donating clothing to the homeless, and visiting a sick friend. Record responses on the board or large sheet of paper under the heading "Individuals.")

Wrapping Up

Closing Activity

Share this quote from *Simon Peter* with the group.

> "Jesus' love for us was demonstrated by his death on the cross. Our love for him is demonstrated by our care for others. This is what Jesus was teaching in John 15:8 when he said, 'My Father is glorified when you produce much fruit and in this way prove that you are my disciples.' And what was the fruit he was looking for? He tells us in verse 12, 'Love each other just as I have loved you' " (page 124).

Ask:

- How has your love for Christ empowered you to love others in Christ's name?
- How has your love for Christ and others produced fruit for the kingdom of God?

Closing Prayer

As a group, pray together the prayer from the end of chapter 5. As an alternative, lead the group in the following prayer:

Holy and forgiving God, we thank you for Simon Peter. We thank you for the gift of forgiveness and second chances. It is not easy for us to confess our sin. It is not easy for us to admit when we are wrong. Grant us wisdom to recognize our sin. Grant us courage to lay our sin before you. Open our hearts to your forgiveness and your love. Go with us into our communities, our workplaces, our churches, and our homes as we fulfill your call to love each other. Amen.

6

THE REST OF THE STORY

Planning the Session

Session Goals

Through conversation, activities, and reflection, participants will:

- recognize the presence of the Holy Spirit in Peter's life,
- identify the key points in Peter's sermons and witness about Jesus Christ,
- discover how Peter faithfully lived out his call to be the "rock" on which Jesus said he would build his church,
- and discern the presence of the Holy Spirit in their own lives.

Biblical Foundation

Acts 2:1-41

Before the Session

- This session plan for chapter 6 offers more material than the session plans for the previous chapters. Keep in mind the time frame you have available and the interests of your group as you choose the discussion questions and activities you want to do.

- The "Book Study and Discussion" focuses on the first five chapters of Acts and concludes with an activity related to writing an "elevator speech" about your faith.
- The "Closing Activity" is based on the final section of chapter 6 titled "Fishing for People" (page 160).
- The "Optional Activities" include ideas for discussing Peter's experiences recorded in Acts 8–12, the final years of Peter's life, and the New Testament letters 1 Peter and 2 Peter.
- Set up a table in the room with name tags, markers, Bibles and extra copies of *Simon Peter* if these will be needed.
- Have a whiteboard or chart paper and markers or a chalkboard and chalk available for recording participants' responses during the session.
- On a board or large sheet of paper write the heading "Peter's Witness." This will be an important tool throughout the Book Study and Discussion.

Getting Started

Opening Activities

Greet participants as they arrive. If there are newcomers allow a short time for introductions.

Share any housekeeping items that need repeating. (See the list for session 1.) Remind participants to respect a policy of confidentiality within the group.

Leading into the Study

Call attention to Hamilton's opening comments for chapter 6 and his observation that Peter changed after Jesus' resurrection.

Read Acts 1:1-11. Explain that Luke, the Gospel writer, is also the author of Acts.

Invite a volunteer to reread Jesus' words in Acts 1:8:

> *"Rather, you will receive power when the Holy Spirit has come*
> *upon you, and you will be my witnesses in Jerusalem, in all*
> *Judea and Samaria, and to the end of the earth."*

Explain that the Hebrew word *ruah* or *ruach* in the Old Testament and the Greek word *pneuma* in the New Testament may both be translated as Spirit, wind, and breath. Ask:

- What does the Holy Spirit do in a person's life? (Invite participants to refer to the section titled "Waiting in the Upper Room" in chapter 6 as they respond to this question.)
- How many people were waiting together in Jerusalem for God's gift of the Holy Spirit? (Acts 1:15 reports there were "about one hundred twenty persons.")
- What were Christ's disciples doing while they waited in this upper room? (Acts 1:14 says "all were united in their devotion to prayer.")

Opening Prayer

Holy and Loving God, we thank you for your disciple Peter. We see in Peter a great example of your power and your willingness to use us, flaws and all, to serve you and spread the gospel of Jesus Christ. Be with us during this session. Open our hearts and our minds to the presence of your Holy Spirit. Guide and direct us to do your will. Amen.

Learning Together

Video Study and Discussion

Play the DVD, then invite the group to discuss the following questions:

- Peter's proclamation of Jesus took him to Joppa, Caesarea Maritima, and Rome. How does your response to Jesus' call take you to new places and experiences?

- How do you think Simon Peter felt when he was in prison in Rome? How does seeing the Mamertine prison help you better understand Peter's experience?
- What enabled Peter to be bold enough to preach about Jesus so widely where he'd denied Jesus before?
- How does Peter's story challenge you? How does it inspire you?
- What insights about Peter's life did you gain from the video? What new questions do you have?

Invite the group members to keep the video in mind as you discuss the Bible and the study book in the rest of your session.

Bible Study and Discussion

Pentecost

Share these points as noted in the section of chapter 6 titled "Pentecost":

- *Pentecost* is a Greek word and means fifty days.
- *Shavuot* is a Hebrew word and means weeks.
- On the Jewish calendar there are fifty days or seven weeks between the celebration of the Passover and the celebration of Shavuot.
- "Passover commemorates the night God delivered the Israelites from slavery in Egypt" (page 131).
- Hamilton notes that Jesus transformed the meaning of the seder or Passover meal to a celebration of the new covenant. As Christians we celebrate the new covenant when we participate in the sacrament of Holy Communion.
- Shavuot commemorates God giving Moses the Ten Commandments on Mount Sinai. It was also a celebration of the harvest in early summer and the giving of the first fruits to God.
- On the day of Pentecost described in Acts 2, Jerusalem was crowded with Jews who had come to celebrate Shavuot.

Invite a volunteer to read Acts 2:1-4. Explain that in this moment Jesus' promise of God's Holy Spirit was fulfilled. Ask:

- How do you think Jesus' followers felt when they realized they had indeed received God's gift of the Holy Spirit?
- What did they immediately do?

Book Study and Discussion

The Day of Pentecost

Invite six volunteers to read the remaining verses of Acts 2 as follows:

- Reader 1: Acts 2:5-13
- Reader 2: Acts 2:14-21
- Reader 3: Acts 2:22-28
- Reader 4: Acts 2:29-36
- Reader 5: Acts 2:37-41
- Reader 6: Acts 2:42-47

Ask:

- How is the Peter in this Scripture passage different from the Peter who denied knowing Jesus on the night of Jesus' arrest?
- What has happened in Peter's life to give him the confidence to boldly preach the sermon recorded in Acts 2?
- What does Peter proclaim about God and Jesus in this sermon? (List these on the board or large sheet of paper with the heading "Peter's Witness." You will refer back to this several times during the session.)
- What was the reaction of the crowd to the disciples' witness and Peter's sermon?
- What did Peter mean when he said, "Change your hearts and lives" (Acts 2:38)?
- How does Luke, in Acts 2, describe the early church? (Acts 2:42-47)

Healing the Crippled Man

Invite three volunteers to read Acts 3 as follows:

- Reader 1: Acts 3:1-10
- Reader 2: Acts 3:11-16
- Reader 3: Acts 3:17-26

Ask:

- How did the crippled man respond to being healed in the name of Christ?
- How did the Israelites respond to the crippled man being healed?
- What does Peter proclaim about God and Jesus in this sermon? (Call attention to the list you started under the heading "Peter's Witness" during the discussion of this question in relation to Acts 2. Circle the points that Peter repeats and add any new points. Emphasize the repetition of the call in Acts 3:19 to "Change your hearts and lives!")

Call attention to Hamilton's observation that each one of us is in some way "spiritually broken, crippled, lame" (see the section titled "Miraculous Healing, Holy Boldness," pages 134–139). Invite volunteers to share an experience of spiritual or physical healing.

Courageous Peter

Invite participants to skim Acts 4:1-22 and respond to the following questions. Ask:

- What happened to Peter and John?
- What question did the leaders and authorities ask Peter and John? (Acts 4:7)
- How does Peter answer? (Acts 4:8-12)
  - ◊ Call attention to the phrase "inspired by the Holy Spirit" (verse 8).

◊　Compare Peter's proclamation about God and Christ with the points already listed on the chart "Peter's Witness" and add any new points.

- What surprised the council and why? (Acts 4:13)
- How is Peter a changed person in this encounter compared to the night he denied knowing Jesus?

Hamilton highlights two Scripture passages from Acts 5 that report the growth of the early church and the leadership of the apostles. Read, or invite volunteers to read, Acts 5:14-16 and Acts 5:41.

Write an Elevator Speech

Invite participants to turn to the section titled "Miraculous Healing, Holy Boldness" in chapter 6. Note Hamilton's suggestion that Christ's followers prepare an "elevator speech." The purpose of the "elevator speech" is to express "a brief description of your faith and how it makes a difference in your life" (page 138). Read the Scripture passage from 1 Peter that Hamilton cites in this section: "Whenever anyone asks you to speak of your hope, be ready to defend it. Yet do this with respectful humility, maintaining a good conscience" (1 Peter 3:15-16).

Invite participants to create small groups of from two to four people. Offer these instructions:

- Create an outline for an "elevator speech."
- Refer to the list we compiled on the chart titled "Peter's Witness" as a place to start.
- Remember Hamilton's purpose for the elevator speech, to express "a brief description of your faith and how it makes a difference in your life."
- If time permits, encourage individuals to share specific examples or experiences of Christ's presence in their lives that may be incorporated in their own elevator speech.

Allow time for each small group to share its outline.

Encourage participants to compose and practice their own elevator speeches as a follow-up to this course, so they will feel more comfortable sharing their faith with others.

Optional Activities

"Beyond Jerusalem"—Miracles of Healing

Invite participants to turn to the section of chapter 6 titled "Beyond Jerusalem" (pages 139–142). As Peter fulfills Jesus' call to fish for people (Luke 5:10), he finds that travel is involved as he follows God's leading to "go fishing" outside the walls of the Holy City. In this section, Hamilton mentions two passages of Scripture related to the growth of the early church and God's miracles of healing.

Read Acts 8:14-17. A key point here is that the church is growing as people hear and accept the Word of God and then receive the Holy Spirit.

Read Acts 9:32-42. Lead a discussion around Hamilton's observation that God's kingdom comes both when healing occurs and when healing does not occur (see the end of the section titled "Beyond Jerusalem" on pages pages 139–142). Invite individuals to share personal experiences related to this.

"Take and Eat, Peter"

Hamilton identifies the story in Acts 10:1–11:18 as "the hinge point not only of the Book of Acts, but of the entire Christian faith" (page 147). It is the story of Peter, a Gentile centurion named Cornelius, and the Jewish food laws.

Instruct participants to scan the story in Acts 10:1–11:18 or invite volunteers to read the story aloud.

Ask:

- What happens in this story? (Write the events on a board or large sheet of paper.)
- Why was this a troubling experience for Peter?
- What did Peter learn from this experience?
- How did the church in Jerusalem initially react?

- What did the church in Jerusalem conclude after hearing Peter's firsthand account of his experience? (Acts 11:18)
- What can we learn from this story today?

Peter's Final Years

In the closing sections of chapter 6, Hamilton offers a wealth of information about the final years of Peter's life, including his interaction with the Apostle Paul, conflicts within the early church, and traditions surrounding Peter's death. You may want to select Scripture texts, quotes, and topics from these sections that you know will be of special interest to your group and offer time for discussion of these during the session.

Wrapping Up

Closing Activity

Read the closing section of chapter 6, "Fishing for People." Ask:

- In what ways will you continue to cast your net and fish for people? (Responses may include participation in various church and community ministries and also individual endeavors.)
- How has your heart and life been changed (paraphrase of Acts 2:38) as a result of this study of *Simon Peter*?

Closing Prayer

Pray the prayer at the end of chapter 6 in *Simon Peter* together.